FROM A MESS TO A
MIRACLE
MY PROCESS WASN'T MY PERMANENT POSITION

PASTOR KIMBERLY KING

Presented to

_____

From

_____

All scripture reference are from the New King James Version of the Bible unless otherwise stated.

ISBN: 978-1-943409-99-0

Published by Pure Thoughts Publishing, LLC

2055 Gees Mill Rd #316 | Conyers, GA 30013 USA

470-440-0875 | www.purethoughtspublishing.com

Printed in the United States of America

DEDICATION AND THANKS

This book is dedicated to every broken girl that may feel she is a mess right now. This book is dedicated to you because I 'm a firm believer that because Christ delivered, freed, and released me; He will surely do the same for you. I also dedicate this book to my grandmother Earline Wilson despite the mess that I constantly found myself in, she knew that one day, I would be here.

Thanks to everyone that played a part with the mess, rather you helped to put me in it, rather you prayed while I was in it, or you helped to pull me out;

Thank you. Special thanks to Pastor Betty Graham for knowing that something was different about me, and an incredible special thanks to Apostle Carl Parrott and my A-Team (Accountability Team). For you all saw what was inside and pushed me to greater. Most importantly my three wonderful children T'darius, Zakeia and Corey Dashon for pushing me and reiterating to me that I have a voice that needs to be heard. To my husband Corey, that came into my life during the most crucial times of my mess and still decided to stand – Thank you! I love you all.

TABLE OF CONTENT

INTRODUCTION

As a little girl, I always felt that church was the place where everything was ok. I felt being in Jesus, there was no problems, no trials, no heartaches, - no mess. From the eyes of a little girl, you see people shouting, falling under the anointing, and speaking in tongues but that little girl did not understand the purpose behind the praise, the purpose behind the fall, nor the purpose behind the intimacy with Jesus. It looked to her that people were being engulfed and surrendering to the true fellowship of Jesus- all while she was a mess.

Loving Christ was a foundation taught and instilled in me by my grandmother Earline, but the understanding of the producing of a miracle was never a thought-out process seen from the eyes of a child that just wanted peace, love, and Christ. The mess to a miracle helps me to understand the mess, understand that my mess was my process, even understanding that I had to come to the realization that the mess was not my permanent place, but it was birthing a miracle-Me; The Generational Curse Breaker, The Warrior, The Pastor, The Prophet, The Region Assassinator.

I lost my sense of trust, honesty, and compassion. I crashed down and became what I consider an emotional mess. I've never been so miserable in whole life. I just wanted to go to bed and never get up.

Shania Twain/Canadian Music

CHAPTER 1

Understanding the mess
Knowing what mess looks like

The webster dictionary defines mess as a person or thing that is dirty, untidy, or disorder. Many times, when one think of mess, we do not look at the filth, the stench, or deformation of the original piece before it was contaminated. All we see is that this is not right, I do not like it, and something needs to be done. Many times, we do not even consider the consequences, affects, nor disruption that mess causes; all we know is that this is mess, or I am a mess.

When the prodigal son found himself in the pig's pen (Luke 15:15-16) from the first sight he did not even comprehend the mess he now made a reality. I can only imagine how he must have felt being in a place where he is being dumped on. A place where others come to look down on him. A place where mud and waste reside but is now looking to him as a place of comfort. He is in a place where he is eating the scraps from what others have thrown away as garbage. The prodigal son found himself in a place that was filthy, with a stench, where the pigs ate, waddled, walked, and even released their waste; and yet he is in this place that he had now found to be his realism.

From the age of 7 to 15 I felt I found myself in a pig's pen. Being touched by various men for their own sexual gratification yet a child wondering day after day; night after night why me? It did not matter where I turned; I was being violated and it seemed no one was there to free me, no one was there to help me, no one was there to save me. There were times I asked God what did I do to deserve this. There were times I would pray so hard and profusely that I would run out of words to say.

I was a mess.

The mess of being violated birth rejection, low self-esteem, unworthiness, unloved, the odd ball, no self – confidence, looking for love in the wrong places, but most of all it caused me not to even love myself.

The mess of being physically and mentally abused birth fear, unresponsiveness to pain, rebellion, and brokenness.

Because of this birthing, I became the little girl that many called fast, the hot momma; even given the stigma that she would be pregnant by 16. I became the little girl that cried everyday and every night just wanting to be love and not have someone to touch her. I became the little girl that tried snorting baking soda at age 13- not realizing nothing was going to happen but she just wanted a way out. I became that little girl that contemplated suicide at age 8. I became that little girl that felt no one liked her because everyone was touching her. I became that defiant little girl that was silently crying out for help just wanting someone to hear her. I became that little girl that would wear the revealing clothing because she wanted someone to pay attention to her and not just see her. I became that little girl that went from man to man looking for real love and not just a sexual touch; I knew what that felt like. I became that little girl that struggled with her sexuality because I felt surely another woman would love me better than this. I became that little girl that felt everyone was looking down on her. I became that little girl that hated being around men because she just knew that whomever they were, they were going to touch her inappropriately. I became that little girl who felt she was in the pig pen; nothing but garbage.

All because I was a mess

Being touched and groped by men that were older than me caused a since of shame. I felt violated and broken. Being looked at with the eyes of seduction at the age of seven from men made me cringed in my seat. The breath of a man became one of my worst nightmares because those breathes were the ones that was a constant reminder of me being touch unwillingly. Being told by men that by me allowing them to touch me and they would in turn buy me gifts; in a sense caused me to prostitute my own body. I was often disgusted by the look of a man that I would often sleep with three sheets three blankets and two spreads on my bed at night. The smell of their cologne would cause me to be ashamed of my very own body. I would not get undressed in front of anyone even at the age of 25. I tried everything I could to protect my body and yet at times it felt like it was to no avail. Many may ask well why didn't you tell anyone, why would you keep something so dreadful a secret, how did you keep something so long and no one not know? Well, the thought of being blamed that it was my fault, being told that if you tell anyone you would be beaten, the thought of being the problem and not the victim was always the music that played within my ears.

Besides, growing up within many African American homes we were taught at an early age - what goes on within the house stays in the house not knowing that there was excruciating pain that was being suppressed within and out of the house. Nonetheless, I am now at a point where I can see and understand that going from one mess to another was like going from bad to worse as my grandmother would say it.

All because I was a mess

Although I didn't grow up in the house with my father' I loved him more than anything. He was the one that made me feel like I was somebody, he did not see my body, but he saw the child that he probably thought had no worries in the world. March of 1993, he brought me a bicycle for my birthday. I was overjoyed. Because of his love for me, he got on the bicycle behind me telling me to pedal Kimmie; pedal and keep straight. In my head, I thought nooooooooo not my father to. Instead of enjoying the moment with my father, I was there thinking that this was going to be another day in the pig pen. I was so afraid because here was another man- but not one time did he inappropriately touch me; not one time did he make an inappropriate advancement towards me. Only God knew how I felt at this very moment. To be this close to a man and not have him touch me. Even now, I cry because my father loved me for real. May of this same year, I got into trouble for going down the street to visit someone without permission, so I had to go to the laundromat with my grandmother. I had no idea this would be the last time I saw my father. Orchestrated by God; yes, it was. When we drove up, there he was. We went inside of the store together; we hugged, we laughed, I gave him my school picture that I had just taken, and I said I love you daddy. Why I had that picture that day; only God knows. I did not think in a million years that that would be the last time I saw the only man that I knew loved me for real. July 1993, the only man that ever loved me for real was burned in a house fire. That was the next beginning of my mess- the worst day of my entire life. I was numb standing there watching my father's house in smoke. For the next several months I would ask my mother to drive me through there just so I could see if it was real, just so I could walk through the rummage to see if there was any clue of him staging this and running away, and just so I could see if my father was really gone. I still remember his address to this day- 411 Bay Street Bishopville SC 29010. I felt like Job. I had lost everything and what else is there to live for? Where would I go now to feel safe, where would I go to find peace? The book of Job talks about Job losing everything and I am not sure if he felt like he was in a mess, but I knew for sure

I was a mess.

After losing my father, I felt things got worst. I was already struggling in school;

I repeated the 6th grade and now with no hope I am spiraling down skid row not even having the mind or desire to become a high school graduate. All I wanted was love because there was that lack. I cried every single day begging God to take my life. I would cry at school, I would cry at church, I would cry standing beside the road. Wherever I could talk with God I cried because this was not fair- So I thought. At the age of 15 ½ the molestation finally stopped. Whewwww; still

I was a mess.

Nonetheless two-years after the death of my father I became pregnant and gave birth to this beautiful little boy. No, the father was not one of the molesters, but it was not any better. While this baby was birthed out of what I thought was love, it turned out to be another mess for me. It seemed as if I was destined to fail and fall. While being pregnant I was told everyone will know your business now. Little did they know that the pregnancy was not even 1/3 of my business. That was a willing touch of my body; what about all the other times when I did not want to be touched? Still, not even thinking, I remember going to the corner store one day and having on a jean jumper that said Used. For the very first time in my life, I felt someone noticed me. The owner of the store called me close to her and said, "Kim I do not care that you have had a baby; you are not used." I did not feel used because of the baby, I felt used because I felt my body was not even my own. Although that built me up just for that few moments, a few days later an individual of spiritual authority said, "You will never find a man to love you for you." When people say that words do not hurt-they lied. Not only do they hurt, but they also stay with you until the curse is broken. It is always the negative words that hold more weight.

So here I am an 18- year- old nothing with a child. Barely making it through school, living on her own, raising her baby brother, father gone, but vowing that no one will ever hurt my baby like I have been hurt. Often one's mess does not look like or smell similar; it still hurts, can cause you to become stagnate, and often kill the destiny within you if you are not careful. Remember John 10:10 -The enemy comes but to still to kill and to destroy but I come that you might have life and have life more abundantly. While mess does not look or feel good, can we truly define what mess looks like, can you identify the purpose of the mess, and can you use mess as your ministry.

Reflections

How did your mess look to you and how did it make you feel?

_____

_____

_____

_____

_____

_____

_____

_____

_____

_____

_____

_____

_____

No matter your position, circumstances, or opportunities in life, you always have the freedom of mind to choose how you experience interpret and ultimately shape your world.

Brendon Burchard

CHAPTER 2

The mess was my process and not my permanent position

Knowing the difference between the process and the position

The dictionary defines process as a series of actions or operations conducing to an end. A permanent position is considered a place where one becomes comfortable and decides to stay. Thus, when I now look at the process verses the position, I understand to become who God has called you to be, there must be some tearing down, some rebuilding, some brokenness, some restoring, and some; I almost gave up and some reviving. As stated in Chapter 1, mess can be viewed from various angles. Oftentimes people especially women; when there has been an excessive amount of mess or they have been standing in it for an extended period of time; begin to believe that we are in too deep and there is no hope of changing. So then, we make our mess our permanent position instead of a place of experience to gain wisdom and knowledge with movement.

The mess was my process and not my permanent position

I often think of Joseph and how God revealed to him his purpose but not the process. Through my mess, I have learned that every assignment and purpose even with life has a process. Many may ask, what was the purpose of the molestation. At the time I really did not understand but I now pin it to the process of being the vessel that God created me to be. It was not just the process of getting there but the enemy saw that one

day I, yes, I would be a threat to his king-
dom and decided that he needed to con-
taminate me, rob me of my innocence,
and even try to kill who God created me
to be early in life.

Just before my mess began, I remember
at the age of 6 standing in my grand-
mothers' room in front of this figure
that was dressed in all white. He never
said anything but every time I would do
something wrong, he would touch me
with his finger, and it would send an
electric shock through my entire body. I

*11) For I know the thoughts that I think
toward you, says the Lord, thoughts of peace
and not of evil to give you a future and a hope.
nkjv.*

distinctly remember my grandmother calling me, me not answering and being touch by that finger. He followed me to church that night and back to my home after the service was over. Even to this day, I am often reminded of that encounter. Today, I thoroughly understand Jeremiah 29:11. There was always a purpose for my life. At that time, I was not thinking about a purpose or a plan. All I remember asking myself was why did I see him and no one else could. I was just a child and no one in their right mind is going to believe me on this one I know.

While the mess did not feel good, it birthed a prayer life within me, not just a prayer life but the cry of a wailing woman. I learned at an early age how to call on Jesus. I learned how to have that one on one with the father, how to trust him when I did not have anyone else to call on. Because of the mess, I learned early how to make my request known unto God. Although it took a while, I had to understand that although Christ had a purpose for my life, the enemy also devised a plot. The enemy wanted me to continue to feel like I was nothing and that I could never be anything but a sexual opportunity to men, the enemy wanted me to continue to believe that I was worthless, and no one ever noticed me only so God's will would not be completed in my life but

The mess was my process and not my permanent position

The enemy wanted me to stay in bondage- the state of being enslaved. Enslaved to my insecurities, enslaved to my filth, enslaved to my anger, enslaved to my unforgiveness and pain. The enemy knew that if he could keep me in bondage then I would not open my mouth to declare freedom, I would not stomp my feet in victory, and I would not clap my hands in joy.

The mess was my process and not my permanent position

The stench of defeat, the filth of anger, the mind of low self-esteem, and the waste of insecurities was the plot intended by the enemy to kill the destiny and purpose within me. Hence, the journey was not easy but worth it. Looking back, I now realize how God created moments of healing for me. So, when I say Romans 8:28 is a reality to me you must believe me. I did graduate high

> 28) And we know that all things work together for good to those who love God, to those who are called according to His pur-

school as well as graduated with a BA degree from Coker College in December 2011. While I did graduate on time, it was not until years later I entered college and completed within 4 years. That process encouraged me that delay is never a denial. God had a plan for my life. Consequently, the college experience was more than for the degree.

I remember during my last year at Coker taking a substance abuse class and having to journal about a traumatic childhood experience. Whewwwwwww that was healing for me. Through my writing – I was noticed and not just seen. The professor of that class responded everyday to the writings within that journal and not only did she respond, but she afforded me the opportunity to share with the class. Talking is a sense of healing as well.

Remember I often did things to be noticed but now it was not to be noticed but to help someone else. Therefore, within the process I had to learned that although it affected me, I am not to be noticed but to be of help. That class offered me the opportunity to be healed. So, through that I learned you cannot have a message without a mess.

The mess was my process and not my permanent position

Later, God connected me to an individual that would come every day to go for a ride or just to talk to build up my self-esteem. Being told that you would never be anything by various men, being told that you would never find a man to love you for you, being called stupid, a whore, and good for nothing but laying on your back grew into not just words for me but my reality. Those words caused me to view myself as how I felt about myself- a nothing. Those words made me believe that everyone else was prettier than I was, better than I was, more intelligent than I was. Why, because those words entered the portal of my ear gates and took root and grew in my heart. Often, it is the words that we speak that births life and death; Proverbs 18:21. While this person continued for a few years to help mold me, strengthen me, and build me; remember I was a mess. So, often people can do all they can until their time is up, and God will send the next person along. From this individual, I was able to believe in myself, I was able to think good of myself, and I even got to the place where I began to like myself.

Many people believed that one must be perfect to walk into the things that God has called you to do. Well, let me tell

21) Death and life are in the power of the tongue, And those who love it will eat its fruit.

you, I was far from perfect and if the truth be told no where near healed when

I became a mother, the wife, when I became the minster, when I became the armor bearer, when I became the teacher nor when I became the pastor. Yes, I was ministering broken and still a half mess.

> 13)I can do all things through Christ who strengthens me. nkjv.

It was not until 3 years after pastoring that God begin dealing with me about healing and accountability. After an intense training with healing and deliverance service, I formed an

A-Team (Accountability Team) for myself. That team has pushed me to step out of low self-esteem and into Philippians 4:13. The A-Team grants me 3 minutes to cry, pout, and even scream if necessary and after that -times up. This team builds my confidence and strongly pushes me to be all that God has called me to be. Not only are they concerned about the spiritual man but the whole man. Today, I realize that indeed the mess was a process and without the genuine and sincere help, it could have killed me. Many do not survive the mess, and many have aborted assignments because of the mess but I have learned that it is a process and does require competent and effective help. Help that pushes and not hinders, help that builds up and not tears down, help that strengthens and not breaks you, help that will stir and not scar. Not only does the process require help from others but going through and the completion of the process is contingent upon you renewing your mind, you rebuilding your heart, and most of all it requires much prayer, strength, and strategies from God.

Nonetheless becoming stuck within the process is so easy as well. The process produces pain, anger, defeat, unworthiness and so much more. I was just reminded of Hannah. She knew that a promised was made to her, but she had to go through the process. Through her process she was being mocked by Penniah. I can only imagine going through the process of desiring a child but barren

and yet someone close to you not help-
ing but killing your hopes and dreams
was excruciating. However, we must understand that there is purpose within the
pain. Hannah cried out to God. She did
not care who saw her nor what they
must have felt about her, she needed
God to move. In a sense, I would say
this was a wailing woman in pain with a
state of an emergency.

Shortly after the birth of my daughter, I
was riding in the car one day with my
family- I cannot remember the song that
came on the radio, but it began to min-
ister to my spirit, tears began to flow and
I began to cry out to God in despera-
tion. I wanted to feel that experience
that I saw in church as a little girl. I

wanted God to be God to me. I yearn to understand what was so special about me that I had to go through this. I wanted the years of hurt, pain, and betrayal to just go away. I wanted God to just say something to help me understand this mess that I was in. It was that day, my joy was renewed, I had hope and knew that there was purpose for my mess, and I was not to stay here but I was to learn and move. That day it felt like everything was ok and I was going to be ok. That very day I felt that I had to be a highly anointed woman of God. I felt a strength that I had never felt before, and I remember feeling that all the pain that I have endured was not to harm me but to establish the person that

God desire- not the damaged little girl but the warrior, the generational curse breaker, the prophet, the pastor.

The mess was my process and not my permanent position.

Reflections

After understanding that the mess was a process, what unwanted position have you taken and how can you move from it?

_____

_____

_____

_____

_____

_____

_____

_____

_____

_____

*When you know yourself, you are empowered;
when you accept yourself you are invincible.*

Tina Lifford

CHAPTER 3

The purpose of the mess

It's time to know who you are

Because of my experience, I value Godly wisdom and counsel. I now thoroughly value these components because I understand that it supports the process as well as having someone there to just talk with to share that this is hard, seems very unfair, and I need help. While I did not reach out to anyone during the time that I was being processed, I say today that Godly guidance and wisdom offers you the opportunity to lean and depend on God and not one's own emotions, thoughts, or the suggestions of the enemy.

There are many times today that I look back at my process and I thank God that I did not become a prostitute. The emotions and feelings of -I was just another sexual opportunity to men even as a child could have very well been that position for me. I felt that my body was not my own and believe it or not what you start early will continue later. I often praise God because crack, cocaine, heroin, pcp, and alcohol could have been my position. When you think of someone that is hurt, broken, and damage looking for a way out- that was I, but instead I chose to seek God. Do not get me wrong, the thoughts were continuous but that was not my position. My praise has always been and still is, God I thank you for keeping my mind. Growing up as a mess often brought on mental issues that even to this day is frowned upon. Being mentally and physically abused and still having to live through it could have caused a nervous breakdown at any given time. There were times when I thought I was literally losing my mind- but God. That was not my position.

So many times, I thought about suicide because I felt I would have been better off not being here. I felt no one loved me anyway -so why live. There were times I could see myself rolling down into the ditch, there were times when I pictured my funeral, and there were even times when I said let me just drown myself in the bathtub because it was so overwhelming, but that was not my position.

The thought of being incarcerated scares me to death, but as a child I saw myself being there often. There were times when I wanted to kill every man on the earth. Rather you hurt me or not, because you were a man- I wanted you dead. I would rehearse in my mind how I would kill- with gasoline, rat poison, inserting a potato in the tail pipes of cars and so much more -why, because I was hurt, damaged, and broken. Thanks be unto God that was not my position. The process of becoming who God wants you to be will often create or birth some-one else or another position. A painful process will also cause you to feel like you are less than who God destined you to be or cause you not to even know who you are. Therefore, I stand firm on Godly wisdom and Godly guidance because we must understand that our process is not our position.

During the year of 2003, I remember working on a job that I loved. I was so in tune with God at this point of my life that I would dream about the next day events and just how God showed it to me is exactly how it happen. During this season, From a Mess to a Miracle was birthed. God told me to write the story and allow others to know that their process does not define who he has called them to be. So here we are and often man look at what we have done, who we were during the process, as well as who we may become because of the process, but not who he has positioned us to be after the process.

When we look at each person that Christ called to become a disciple, which one was perfect? Not one, but he called each one of them just as he has called you and I. One of the greatest challenges for me has been understanding, knowing, and walking into who God has called me to be- not man but God. I had to realize that the sexual abuse did not call me to be a prostitute nor a whore, but it called me to be a generational curse breaker. The process taught me what signs to look for within girls that could be going through abuse and become that warrior to call it out, address it, and kill it. The process caused me to love on young ladies and let them know that their body belongs to them and no one has the right to touch without their permission. This process afforded me the opportunity to become vigilant, aware, and inquisitive. While it did not look like it to man, my position was not the pig pen but the generational curse breaker.

Due to the lack of discernment and relationship with Christ, many times people call you what the process painted you out to be and not what God called you to be. The process caused me to become a warrior early in life. I did not just war on my behalf, but I warred for my family, I warred for my brothers, I warred for other young girls that could have been going through the same exact process as I was. Many felt that because they saw me crying that that was all I knew to do but little did they know-I cried with them, but I prayed in my closet. I had no choice but to pray because of the severity of my process. Who was going to keep my mind, who was going to keep me free, who was going to intercept the actions that would have caused me to be incarcerated, - Nobody but God. Thus, my process did not position me as a crybaby but a warrior.

The bible declare that gifts come without repentance and it also states that many are called but few are chosen. During my process I did not even know, nor did I ask for this and I surely do not know why he chose or called me, but I will gladly walk in it- at least now anyway. During this process I spent a lot of time praying and talking with God. There were times when I would dream things and it would happen just as he showed me. I never told anyone about these experiences because I was already a mess as is, so I did not need anything else to be hampered over my head- Instead, I just walked it out. My process was never to dim nor silent my voice, but the process was to be the voice for God. This does not mean everyone is called to the office of the prophet it just means you have to know who he has called you to be and walk in it. So, I do not have just any voice, but I echo his voice.

The bible also declares that he gives us pastors after his own heart. I would like to believe that my process was just the beginning of preparing me to become a pastor. It offered me the opportunity to be able to discern not just from actions but from the heart. This process afforded me the opportunity to yield to and see ministry and leaders from a different perspective. It just did not happen as a little girl, but as I grew, there were various times, situations, and occasions where God pointed out to me that he was not just concerned about the shouting, the falling out under the spirit, and the speaking in tongues but he was concerned about the whole man. He convinced me that the church was where you come broken and leaved whole; he reassured me that the church was where you come sick and leave healed; and he continuously proved to me that the leader was one that lead from compassion and not, unjust conviction. So, my process was not just to call me out to be seen or noticed but it was positioning me to be a pastor after God's own heart.

The process is not easy and every call from the process is clearly different. Nonetheless, as an individual you must understand and know who God has called you to be despite the turmoil, afflictions, and pain of the process. I encourage you to not allow the process to cheat you out of God's ordain position for your life. You must know who you are and walk in it- It is imperative. The enemy tried to taint, disqualify, and steal my innocence but Christ came that I may live and live abundantly. While it takes the help of others; it also requires effort, tenacity, and strength from you. You do not have to stay there, and you do not have to become what the process portrayed, but you can get up from there and stand in who God has called you to be. I was a mess, but my process was not my permanent position.

Reflection

How do you define yourself now?

_____

_____

_____

_____

_____

_____

_____

_____

_____

_____

_____

_____

_____

_____

_____

PRAYER OF DECLARATION

Today I bind up the spirit of low self-esteem and declare that you are more than enough.

I bind up the mentality of feeling that you are nothing and declare that Christ has created you on purpose for purpose. I take authority over the generational and regional curse of incest, molestation, and rape, and I declare that you are free from that bondage and every enemy through your bloodline is being pulled down. I call out the weakness of every man that suffer from the trauma of their childhood and now want to violate you;

I speak freedom and deliverance to your heart, mind, and spirit. I speak to that little girl in you that wants peace and love and declare that you will no longer walk-in fear, you will no longer walk-in defeat, you will no longer walk-in abandonment, you will no longer walk-in shame, you will no longer walk-in hurt and brokenness, you will no longer use your body as a tool, but I speak joy and reconciliation over and in your life. I speak to that brokenness within you that you shall be healed and not a statistic of drugs, alcohol, promiscuousness, and prostitution but a woman after God's own heart that will teach and train other girls to be bold and fierce to walk in the things of God as well. I declare that after today your past is no longer a hinderance but a testimony, and you will walk into who God has called you to be – you are the generational curse breaker, you are the voice of healing, you are the warrior that will tear down and rebuild, you are the power pusher. I declare and decree that your process is no longer your permanent position, but I call forth the woman to come alive in you, come alive from the grave, come alive from the mess, come alive from the agony of defeat, come alive from the thoughts and words of others for your process was not to kill you but to align you. I speak stirring to every ministry within your belly and call forth wholeness to complete all that is assigned to you. Amen!

ABOUT AUTHOR

Kimberly King is a wife, mother, Special Education Teacher, Ministry Coach, and Pastor of Restoration Word Ministry. She's a 1997 graduate of Mt. Pleasant High School, holds a BA Degree from Coker College and a Masters from Walden University. Kimberly is the founder of Restoration Word Ministry, Center of H.O.P.E. as well as Restoration House. She is ambitious, an out of the box thinker, a servant after God's own heart and a visionary who is passionate about the things of God. Kimberly loves God with her entire heart and stands firm on the foundation that in all that you do; do it that God may get the glory.

www.ingramcontent.com/pod-product-compliance
Lightning Source LLC
La Vergne TN
LVHW021622080426
835510LV00019B/2713